Reduce, Reuse, Recycle

Graphs

D1312648

Suzanne Barchers

Publishing Credits

Dona Herweck Rice, *Editor-in-Chief*; Lee Aucoin, *Creative Director*; Don Tran, *Print Production Manager*; Sara Johnson, *Senior Editor*; Jamey Acosta, *Associate Editor*; Lesley Plamer, *Interior Layout Designer*; Stephanie Reid, *Photo Editor*; Rachelle Cracchiolo, M.A.Ed., *Publisher*

Image Credits

cover Cynthia Farmer/ZTS/EdBockStock/Shutterstock; p.1 Cynthia Farmer/ZTS/EdBockStock/Shutterstock; p.4 Randy Plett/iStockphoto; p.5 Art Explosion; p.6 Andre Blais/Shutterstock; p.7 Sandra Kemppainen/Shutterstock; p.9 Gorilla/Shutterstock; p.10 (top left) Mettus/Shutterstock, (top right) Mura/iStockphoto, (bottom left) Dave White/iStockphoto, (bottom right) Nick Barounis/Shutterstock; p.11 (top) Stephanie Reid. (bottom) Todd Bates/iStockphoto; p.12 Ivonne Wierink/Shutterstock; p.13 Monkey Business Images/Shutterstock; p.14 (left) Valentin Agapov/Shutterstock, (right) Hypnotype/Shutterstock; p.15 (left) BMCL/Shutterstock, (middle) Claudio Baldini/Shutterstock, (right) Katrina Leigh/Shutterstock; p.16 SergioZ/Shutterstock; p.17 ZQFotography/Shutterstock; p.18 2happy/Shutterstock; p.19 (left) Pinchuk Alexey/Shutterstock, (right) Gemenacom/Shutterstock; p.20 Paul Prescott/Shutterstock; p.21 (top) Stephanie Reid, (bottom) prism68/Shutterstock; p.22 Stephanie Reid; p.23 Kirill R./Shutterstock; p.24 Newscom; p.25 Gelpi/Shutterstock; p.26 Morgan Lane Photography/Shutterstock; p.27 Corbis/Superstock

Teacher Created Materials

5301 Oceanus Drive
Huntington Beach, CA 92649-1030
http://www.tcmpub.com

ISBN 978-0-7439-0875-7

©2011 Teacher Created Materials, Inc.
Reprinted 2012

Table of Contents

Reduce

November 15 is a special day for our school. It is Warder School Recycling Day. The students and staff plan to work at the 3 Rs of recycling. They are **reduce**, **reuse**, and **recycle**.

REDUCE · RECYCLE · REUSE ·

The students will keep track of their work over the next 5 months. Then they will see how well they have done. They will celebrate on Earth Day in April.

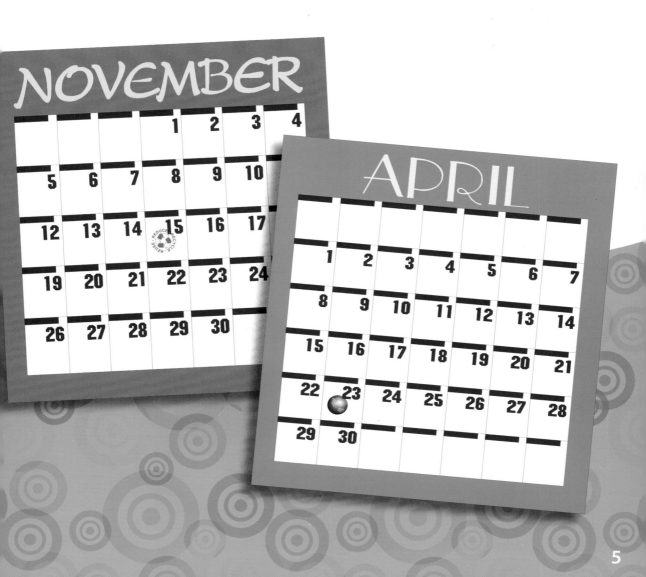

The students start by adding up how many gallons of water they use in a day. Some students take showers. They start timing how long they spend in the shower.

Water Usage (Approximate)

Activity	Water Used
brushing teeth with the water running	1 gallon
washing hands or face	1 gallon
taking a bath	40 gallons
taking a shower	4 gallons per minute
flushing the toilet	4 gallons
washing clothes	10 gallons
running the dishwasher	20 gallons

The students keep track of how often they flush the toilet. They also count how many gallons of water they use for other activities. Now they add up what they have counted.

LET'S EXPLORE MATH

Look at the **chart** and answer the questions.

a. Jordan spends 10 minutes in the shower. How much water does she use?

b. Jordan brushes her teeth with the water running 3 times each day. How much water does she use each day?

The students use about 68 gallons of water each day. They graph the **data** from their chart to see which activities use the most water.

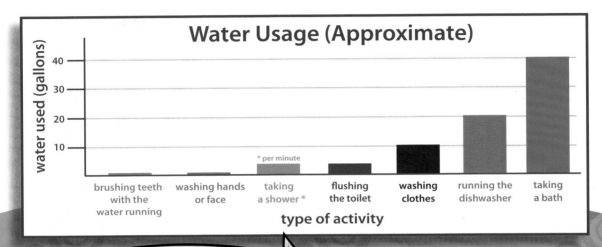

Water Usage (Approximate)

y-axis: water used (gallons)

x-axis: type of activity

brushing teeth with the water running | washing hands or face | taking a shower * | flushing the toilet | washing clothes | running the dishwasher | taking a bath

* per minute

LET'S EXPLORE MATH

Look at the graph above. Then, answer the questions.

a. Which activity uses the most water?

b. How much more water is used to run the dishwasher than to wash clothes?

c. Which activities use equal amounts of water?

Then the students think of ways they can use less water. They can turn off the water while brushing their teeth. They can turn off the water when they rub soap on their hands. They can spend less time in the shower.

Next the students look at their lunches. Some students bring their lunches to school. The food in their lunches often comes in packages. The students make a list of the items that come in packages.

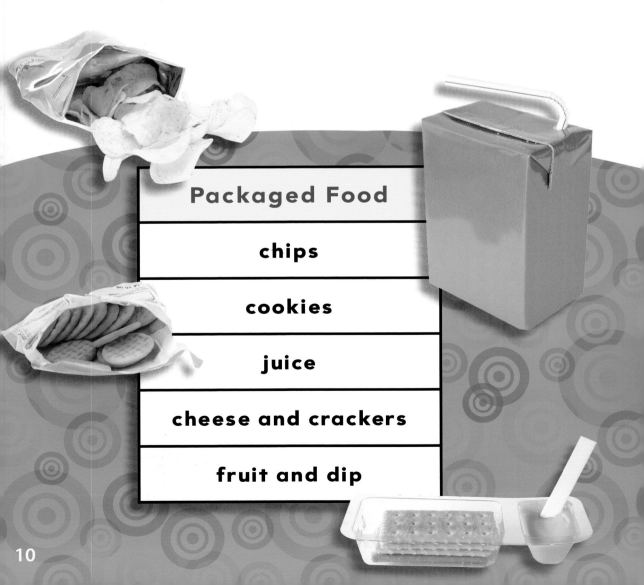

Packaged Food
chips
cookies
juice
cheese and crackers
fruit and dip

Some students get lunch in the cafeteria. Their forks and straws are wrapped in plastic. Their milk comes in paper containers. The trash for the class nearly fills up one trash can!

The students plan to have a no-trash lunch. They use lunch boxes or tote bags. They put their food and drinks in reusable containers. The students who buy their lunches bring forks and spoons from home.

Reuse

The students were able to reduce trash with their no-trash lunch. Next, the students do some research. They learn how smart it is to reuse things. They find out that there are many items that can be reused.

The students decide to empty out the trash can. They sort the trash into piles. Most of the trash is paper. A lot of the paper is nearly blank. They decide to reuse paper more often.

Tree and Paper Usage for 30 Students

Sheets of Paper Used Each Day per Student	Number of Trees Used Each Day
5	3
10	6

Some of the trash includes things like paper clips and rubber bands. They make a list of ways to reuse some things.

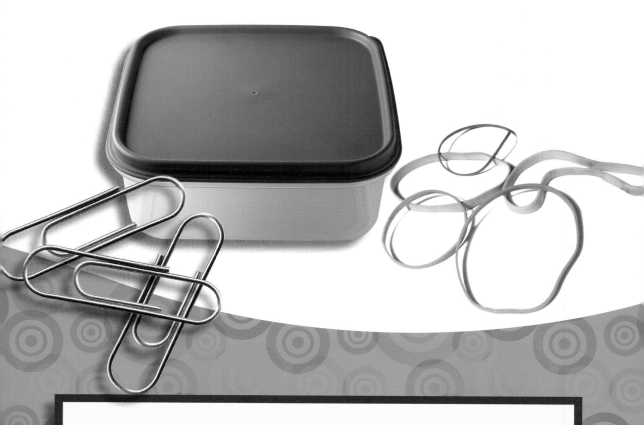

Ways to Reuse Trash

- Write on the front and the back of paper.
- Cut up paper for note paper.
- Save paper clips in a box.
- Save rubber bands in a box.
- Use a cloth instead of paper towels.

Recycle

The students learn about **landfills** next. Landfills are places where trash is taken. There are rules about how the trash is handled.

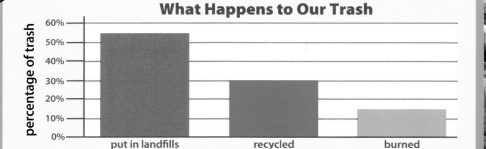

What Happens to Our Trash

The **bar graph** shows where trash goes. Look at the graph and answer the questions.

a. Where does most of the trash go?

b. What percentage is recycled?

16

A lot of trash ends up in landfills because people do not sort it. Much of it can be recycled. The students want to find out what type of recycling will help most.

The students do some more research. They learn that paper takes up the most space in a landfill. Recycling paper seems like a good place to start.

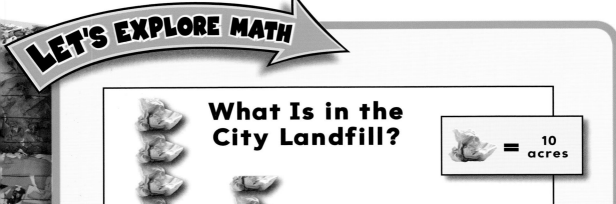

What Is in the City Landfill?

= 10 acres

paper   food and yard waste   metal   glass   plastic

The **pictograph** shows what is in 1 landfill. Look at the graph and answer the questions.

a. Paper takes up most of the space in a landfill. What takes up the next largest amount of space?

b. What kinds of trash each take up equal amounts of space?

18

The students bring in stacks of newspapers from home. Each week they weigh the newspapers. The first week they collect 200 pounds. The next week they collect another 200 pounds.

After 10 weeks the students have 2,000 pounds of paper. That is 1 **ton**! Their parents take it to a recycling center. The recycled paper saves about 17 trees.

The students keep bringing in newspapers to recycle. They also learn ways to reuse the paper. For example, they shred some of the newspapers to use in their school garden.

The students put the strips of paper around the plants and cover them with some dirt. This helps keep the weeds from growing. It also helps keep the plants moist. That saves water, too.

The recycling center does not pay for newspapers. But it pays for cans and plastic bottles. The students start to bring cans and bottles to school, too. They make a pictograph to chart how many pounds of cans and bottles they collect.

Cans and Plastic Bottles for Recycling

 = 25 pounds

cans

plastic bottles

The students go to the recycling center to turn in the cans and bottles for money. They save all the money they get.

LET'S EXPLORE MATH

Look at the chart. Then answer the questions.

Buyback Recycling Center Payments for Cans and Plastic Bottles		
Number of pounds	Total payment for cans	Total payment for bottles
100	$125	$100
200	$250	$200
300	$375	$300
400	$500	$400

a. How much would the students make if they brought in 300 pounds of cans?

b. Will the students make more money if they bring in 200 pounds of cans or 200 pounds of plastic bottles?

The students will use the money for their Earth Day party. They are surprised at how fast the money adds up!

The students have a new problem. They cannot spend all the money on a party. They have too much money. But they have worked hard, and they want to celebrate Earth Day.

Their principal comes up with a great idea. They can plant trees in front of the school. Then, every day will feel like Earth Day!

A Mountain of Trash

The students at Hollis School want to recycle more. The chart below shows an example of how many pounds of trash a family of 4 throws away each week. The students can use the chart to make a graph to help them plan how to recycle more.

Weekly Trash for Family of Four

Kind of Trash	Pounds Thrown Away
paper	30
food	30
metals	10
glass	10
plastics	10
other	10

Solve It!

a. Use the data in the chart to make a bar graph.

b. Which 2 kinds of waste make the most trash?

c. What types of trash do you want to recycle?

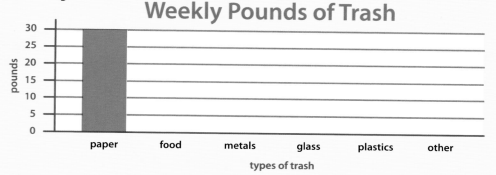

Weekly Pounds of Trash

Use the steps below to help you solve the problems.

Step 1: Draw a graph like the one above.

Step 2: Look at the chart. Then, add a bar for food.

Step 3: Look at the chart. Then, add a bar for metals, glass, plastics, and other.

Step 4: Look at the graph. Find the 2 bars that make the most trash.

Glossary

approximate—an estimate or close amount

bar graph—a graph that uses bars to show information

chart—information that is put in columns and rows so that it is easy to read

data—a collection of information

landfill—a place where trash is taken and stored

pictograph—a graph that uses pictures and symbols to show information

recycle—to process something so it can be used again

reduce—to use less of something

reuse—to use something more than once

ton—2,000 pounds

Index

Let's Explore Math

Page 7:

a. 40 gallons

b. 3 gallons

Page 8:

a. taking a bath

b. 10 more gallons

c. brushing teeth and washing hands or face

Page 16:

a. Most of the trash goes to a landfill.

b. 30%

Page 18:

a. food and yard waste

b. metal, glass, and plastic

Page 24:

a. $375

b. The students will make more money if they bring in 200 pounds of cans.

Solve the Problem

a.

b. paper and food

c. Answers will vary.